<u>*WATER*</u>

Written By: Reign Billings Sr.
Copyright 2020

Intro

I want to start off each new year by going something BIG to make my son's life much better than it was the year before..

Hospital Room

I'm alone
Sitting here in this hospital room
Alone, just on my own
Overlooking this lake
That's as still as the stars
Lights from passing cars
Illuminate my view
As I decide what to do
With my next steps
These pains, like time
Slowly crept in my chest
Found them a spot
And gave me their best
But the pains I sustained
Wasn't wise enough to see
I'm a fighter, a warrior
I'll never concede

Smiles & Laughter

Putting on a smile
Through the needle sticks
The constant pain
Trying to fill myself with laughter
So the tears won't rain
But so much is trying to takeover
As i'm feeling so drained
So much constant strain
How is my body still standing
Since birth
So much has been asked of me
My life has been so demanding
I'll never be free
Though I withstood all it gave
And gave back all I could give
I'm just trying to hold on
I'm just trying to live

<u>So Worn</u>

The passion in my belly
Can't be taught
With it, I was born
There's been so little structure
My life is torn
My body is so worn
I do my best to be strong
Can't let em see me weak
They could take my passion all wrong
I write so I speak
I continue to live in the dark
I haven't seen light in so long
Even my shadow stays hidden
It has problems of its own

Insight

Freeing my thoughts
And my pains alike
There's so much within
That I release when I write
It's so much insight
In the words I release
So much that can be learned
So much I could teach
I do hold a lot in
Though there's so many I could reach
I'll never stop writing
There's still so much to unleash

Passion Gives Passion

Your passion
Gives me passion
It's that light that I need
Your love digs in me deep
Now my body can feed
Just when i'm feeling weak
You give me the strength I need
Pain digs in me daily
But you give me
The fulfillment to smile
When we're touching
I'm constantly blushing
My heart hasn't beat
This way in a while
If you stand strong by my side
I'll do what I can for you
No, i'm not the best
But i'll do my best for you

Fragile

Just hold me
In your arms
As I give
This fragile heart
To you

<u>This Dream</u>

I saw you in a dream
I had no idea what it mean
But you had the softest wings
So it would seem
They kept me so warm
My heart was so torn
And your kisses during the storm
Helped to heal this man
I was battered and bruised
So used, so abused
But the scene in this dream
Was like none other
Your true passion blanketed me
It draped over me like a cover
I felt so wanted
Now my body hovers
I needed this so much
The slightness of your touch
And now my heart races
The moment our lips touch

<u>Vision In The Dark</u>

Meditating in the dark
Cause even the light hides evil
It's hiding within kindness
But it basks in all people
The darkness helps me see
What the light has hidden
I dig deep within myself
It's there I have the visions
I can see what others can't
In the shadows of the day
Most don't understand
But it's how I find my way
Through the pain & the strain
How I keep a smile on my face
In order to keep forward
I have to go to a deeper place

<u>Circle Maze</u>

I look inside me
Because I have no one beside me
Alone yet again
No love, no friends
Trying to move on
But I keep ending up
Where I began
My path is a circle
A round maze full of doubt
I'm constantly looking within me
Trying to find a way out

<u>Written</u>

How come
Plans don't stand as written
There's so much to mention
But no one's ready to listen
My dreams are written
Mainly in my mind
Money is the issue
So i'm coming up short
On my grind
Well, the lack thereof
So I watch the clouds
Slowly pass above
Wishing I could reach
Bare hands, no gloves

<u>My Siren</u>

You are my siren
These waters run deep
When I dive in your pond
My entire being flows weak
Just listen when I speak
As I embrace your curves
The way you feel in my arms
Relaxes my nerves
You are my siren
Your voice puts me in a trance
When I gaze into your eyes
I'm floating as in a dance

Take Your Pain

I can't change
The time nor the tide
But I can
Take the pain
Out of your eyes
Let me take you on a ride
Life can be exciting
With much surprise
I'm not perfect
In fact, i'm a mess
My life is full of stress
But i'll push that to the side
To give you all the best

<u>How Should I Feel?</u>

Death may be my calling
But I constantly fight to live
The world feeds me pain
Though i've got so much love to give
How should I feel?
Being alive but dead inside
All they see are smiles
Hiding the death
That lives in my eyes

My Son Grow

I'm thankful to be alive
Just to watch my son grow
There are some things going on
He shouldn't have to face, I know
Life has its ups and downs
It comes and goes with no flow
So I try to keep him
On the right path
Cause the left is a no go
I'm thankful to be alive
To watch him smile each day
I do my best
To be the father he deserves
In every way

<u>Water</u>

Flow with me
Move so fluently
Just grow with me
Be as water
Let's take shape
My love
Just flow with me

<u>How Can I?</u>

How can I write?
About what's right
When all in my life
Is wrong
How can I speak?
On what's in the light
When I don't feel I belong
My body is weak
My body is strong
There's a battle within
No telling which side will win
But it will be a fight til the end
There are so many folks
On the outside looking in
Trying to increase my rage
So I close my eyes, take a breath
And just turn the page
A new chapter
A new beginning
I've moved passed them
In my life
I'm on a path
That only moves forward
No time to stop
No time for strife

<u>My Eyes</u>

I stared at myself in the mirror
And in time I begin to wonder
Are these the eyes of evil
Or is there just evil in my eyes
To my surprise
I couldn't answer the question
That I had placed upon myself
For the life of me
I know there's right in me
Despite the fight in me
There has got to be
Some sort of light in me

Lily Through The Heart

On my knees I begged her
My eyes turned red
From the tears I shed
As I looked upon this queen
This angel from my dreams
Please don't take your smile away
It's my guiding light
But in one quick swoop
She took me for a loop
As she thrust
A flower through my heart
From the lilys
I placed upon her feet
It's over, I fell weak

Picture In A Frame

Picture me perfecting
Every picture in your frame
Folks talking negative about me
But don't even know my name
So much in me has changed
So much is truly different
There's so much I could maintain
As my poetry captures your attention
Every picture in your vision
Isn't what it may seem
Look a little deeper
You'll be enlightened by hidden things
Visuals of things
That we thought we really knew
But so much came to life the older we grew
I can paint a perfect picture
With hidden gems in every stroke
But your mind has to be open
To see it different than other folk
Either way the picture's speaking
Without speaking verbally
Everybody can take a look
And they'll see whatever they see

<u>Strong Verses</u>

I got a fever for the flavor
But the passions all gone
She said she love me
But my heart is all wrong
I'm my own worst critic
That's why my verses so strong
You ain't been through
What i've been through
So you can't understand the mindstate
My visions ain't just dreams
I bring em' to life
Whenever I wake
I may move at a slower pace
But my mind is four steps ahead
I can write a verse for anything
So my son is forever fed

Not That Man

I apologize
For not being the man
You dreamed you'd have
I miss the days
I miss the ways
That I made you smile
I apologize for the tears
All the pain that i've caused
I'm not the man I was
Not that man at all
I'm preparing for death
Though I haven't yet lived
I don't know what's within
But I have little to give
These pains upon me
Are attacking me everyday
Just know i'll always love you
Even when the pain & weakness
Finally take me awa

Gift

If christmas is about gifts
Then i'd love the gift
Of being wrapped within your lust
The gift of your warmth
As my manhood throbs is a must
Thrusting in and out
Of your erotic pleasure
The sounds of ecstasy from your lips
Was beyond any measure

<u>Remember</u>

I'm containing me
Self-containing the things
That's putting a strain
On what's maintaining me
So much is obstructed
So i've constructed
Moments in a timeline
That I can remember
So much is lost
Though i've contained
Some of my coldest nights in December
I'm just trying to keep warm
Without thick thighs or timber
There's just so much
I can't remember

<u>Concealed Weapon</u>

I'm riding
Both of my hands on the wheel
And though my weapon is concealed
I try to give these people
The look, the appeal
That i'm living right
I'm not living completely wrong
But in some of the places that I rome
You've gotta be prepared to stand alone
Against fake ass friends
And these clown ass enemies
Let me focus cause i'm riding
This illegally concealed weapon
Is keeping me protected
As I strive to create a better me
Cause I know when folks
See me break free
They are gonna attack heavily
I'm gonna stay safe
At least, I better be
I'll just keep moving steadily
Until they give me a reason
To make my weapon flex
To a better beat

Laws Of Restraint

Am I still the man I once was
Can I still sustain
An enormous amount of pain
While keeping it contained
As I go on with my day
Or will it attack me in such a way
That I cannot obey
The laws of restraint
I tend to explode
Into a different mode
When my kindness is tested
Though i'm so deeply invested
In staying free
And not have my son see
Me in a solitary place
I never want him to be
The laws of restraint
Don't always work as planned
But I must stand strong
I must become a different man

Train Of Thought

My train of thought has changed
My focus still remains
Just on completely different things
I'm trying to gain patients
The road i'm facing is a long one
Go thing for me
That I am a strong one
Over the next year
I plan to move alone
I plan to take a trip
Into an unknown zone
If anything goes wrong
It could crumble my home
My train of thought has changed
But I still remain
I've shed the shell
Of the man I used to be
I'm slowly getting to a place
Where i'm feeling kind of free
Free from the person
The man I used to be
While trying to grow into this man
I should of been for me

<u>Who Am I Now?</u>

Who am I now?
I'm trying to change
Just reset
But my thoughts are still cloudy
A little blurry at best
Who am I now?
How can I clear this filthy path
Should I take another route
And bypass this aftermath
I'm a man on a mission
So my focus is at attention
I'm on a search for true knowledge
So when folks speak
I do my bes to listen
Sometimes I zone out
Because their speech
Ain't part of my vision
Who am I now?
I'm not really sure
I'm still trying to find myself
Putting my old ways behind
While trying to free myself
Just roaming kind of lost
While still trying to be myself
Who am I now?

<u>Dream</u>

I dream of being
A different man for you
I'm taking a different stand
Because of you
Because of your love
I'm making different plans
I want to make your life better
Be a better man
Than I have in the past
You may have loved & lost
But i'll be your last
Fill you with passion
That no one ever has
Dream at your pleasure
I'll try to make em' come true
Though i'm not the right man
I" do my best for you

<u>Country Queen</u>

She's back!
My vision of loveliness
My country lioness
My country queen
This woman graces my dreams
It's a remarkable scene
Each glance at her
Takes my breath
The love she gives
Is like unimaginable wealth
She's back!
This woman I crave
For her passion, I thirst
Her kisses give me life
Her love brightens my universe
A beautiful treasure
My shining star
I feel her so close
Though she lives so far
Could this be a dream
It seems so real
I wonder if she knows how I feel
Damn, she's back!

Emissary Of Poetry

I am the emissary
The emissary of poetry
On a mission
To unleash her spoken words
From land to land
To plant her exotic beauty
Into the minds of those
Who no longer believe she exists
Her words are true
Her message is powerful
And as her emissary
I will release
What she has bestowed upon me
I am not the only one chosen
There are many emissaries
Many more ambassaders
To plant the seed
Of her artistry
I travel many roads
I explore many unbeaten paths
As I go forth on her behalf

<u>Is This A Game?</u>

I love her
But i'm not sure
If she loves me the same
I'm not sure if this is a game
Or if she truly wants my last name
The passion feels right
But something is wrong
She's a married woman
But I want her as my own
Not seeing her drives me crazy
Wrapped in her arms keeps me sane
I love when she calls me suga bear
And express what's on her brain
Yes, I need her
I want to treat her
Like a queen
Take her on trips around the world
Expose her to all her dreams
I'm a man on a mission
My intentions to make her mine
Anything she can imagine
I'll give to her in time

Love Or Lust

She says that she loves me
But she's constantly reaching for wood
Is it love or lust
Cause she seems up to no good
I don't mind a freaky woman
But stay with dick on the brain
I'm about the pleasures of life
But this chick here is about them games
Does she really love me
Or love me not
I don't know where her hearts at
Her body stay hot for this wood
While her hands and eyes
Is always up to no good

Dance Of The Candle Light

Dance with the light
Let your moves be graceful
Feel the passion flow
From deep within
Once the dance begins
The end of this dance
Is truly unknown
As long as the light glows
The dance
The dance with the light
Will continue to flow
So go on
Groove on
As the light moves on
With true passion
With unimaginable grace

<u>Visualize</u>

How is my visual
Not visualized
You can see what I feel for you
Just look in my eyes
Listen to my voice when I speak
You're not listening
To how I feel
Just makes me weak
I stand before you constantly
Letting all my emotions leak
I'm just getting started
My passion isn't even at its peak
Everyday I wake
I give you all of me
Just visualize what I speak
Or would you rather
I let you be

<u>Nothings Changed</u>

I dream for life to be different
But this bullshit still the same
I try to move in different lanes
Unfortunately ain't shit changed
Am I supposed to be where I am
Should life really be this fucked up
Now a days I feel like i'm stuck
I ain't never had any kind of luck
But they will be quick
To look down on me
If I get in the Chevy
And run a muck
Then I step back
Look at all the facts i'm facing
Back and forward
Cross the floor i'm pacing
There's no need
To put my hand on my chest
Without even checking
I can feel my heart racing

<u>I Am..</u>

I'm nobody
I'm the darkness
I'm a thorn
Being tossed in the trash
So the flower can look
More beautiful
I'm what most folks
Wish didn't exist
Thank you for ignoring me
For pushing me aside
Because i've grown
I've gained knowledge
I've thrived and survived
I appreciate you for creating
That which I became
I am Reign!!!!

Better Way

I hope you wake on this day
In a better way
Than you were yesterday
Today can bring some light
If you look at it right
Hopefully your in a better place
Despite how you were feeling last night
I wish you were in my sight
I'd hold you close
And let you know
You'll be alright
Your safe with me
Bask in this embrace with me
Feel yourself encased in me
I'll help you heal

<u>Needs</u>

My lips need your lips
My body needs your arms
My wood needs your pond
Baby, what is going on?
My hands need that peach
My tongue needs your body
Your the only woman I want
You don't have to be jealous of nobody
My ears need your voice
My heart needs your love
All of me belongs to you
I put that on the stars above

<u>The Game</u>

I'm constantly immersed
In anger and pain
So much hatred still remain
But I try no to play the game
Within me deep
Is the stress and strain
From all of the things
I constantly contain
I live and die in my brain
So with each new day
I hope my life ain't the same
I try to never look back
Moving forward is all I see
So every chance I get
I try to mold a better me

Breathe Life

Does love truly heal
Or just the ones we can't see
I embraced the woman of my dreams
And she healed me
My heart now beats
A passionate melody
I no longer have to exhale
Cause she breathes life into me
Her touch gives me a rush
That only she can contain
It's insane what she makes me feel
The things upon me she has healed
My love for her I can't conceal
So I wear it upon my chest
Like a badge of honor

<u>Carved In Her Skin</u>

She marked her skin
She embedded his name
The name of this man
Who consumes her being
Who inhales her soul
Carved within her body
Is the name of her love
She has released herself
Onto this man
She has given her all
To this street beast
Why him?
Why me?
She has chosen
Her heart and soul agree
This is the man she wants
I am the man she needs

<u>I Woke</u>

This morning I woke
I woke to the sound of her voice
I woke to the smell of you
But my senses
Weren't hearing or smelling true
The absence of you
Triggered the essence of you
Though the presence of you
Was nowhere in the room
My heart skipped beats
Breathing was obsolete
When I could not find you
Within my immediate vicinity
The bed was cold
My soul was alone
I needed to be embraced
Tightly encased within your arms
Your presence is needed
So much of me
Has been depleted
But for now
Your gone

Reading Is A Pathway

I'm writing
Cause reading breeds knowledge
It can begin a pathway
To imagination and greatness
There's a faithness within us
That help us believe in ourselves
Reading is a pathway
There's millions of books upon the shelves
We have to think for ourselves
Create the life we want to live
There will be no handouts
Others will never want to give
I'm still writing
Because the paths i've taken
Has fed me knowledge
Why keep it bottled up
I could help another see their path to college

Imagination

Life is as it be
When the wind blows
Imagination flows
There is where i'll be
Trying to invision things
Only my minds eye can see
Intentionally embracing the things
That set my soul free
I live in this place
It's the one place I best know me
My mind never rests
My imagination is what it be

<u>Impressed By Impressions</u>

I'm impressed by the impressions
That your face have made for me
The way that your voice sounds
Like those moans are just played for me
The way your body shakes and shivers
As though this dance was created for me
The way your passion flows
Like this waterfall was engraved for me
I can feel the heat from your skin
Like this fire was all my own
I'm feeling this pain when your gone
I guess it's my pain to bare alone

<u>Dancing Flame</u>

I watched the flame
I watched as it danced
It seems to just float
Slightly above the wick
It floated and danced for me
Glowing brightly
As it performed
In all its graceful movement
As though it had practiced
This trancing dance for me
It captured me
Motives unknown
But I have gone into thee

<u>Captured</u>

I'm captured
In this life
I've been captured
By something powerful
Something relentless
In its pursuit
It's filled with life
It's bite could ignite
A new man in me
Who set this beast free
Upon an endangered species like me
I'm just there frozen
But I cannot flee
Ambition is attacking me

<u>Hunger</u>

I'm hungry
I try to eat
Dreams
But I woke
With more pains
Body soulfully
Drained
It's getting harder
To contain
A smile inside
There are ideas
In me
Insanely running wild
They need to be
Released
How can I get
Them out

<u>Visions Within Visions</u>

I'm searching
For something else
Not knowing
Which way to go
I'm looking for
Visions within my
Visions
So they're getting
My full attention
I'm a man
On a mission
To become a
Greater being
But my enlightenment
Needs enlightening
Because what i'm
Feeling
I am not seeing

<u>Eating Information</u>

I'm still feeding
Feasting on all
The knowledge
My brain can intake
Books upon books
Videos of information
Anywhere I can feed
I'm eating it up
No hesitation
Knowledge is my
Nutrition
It nurtures my
Lost soul
This quest i'm on
Is starting to
Make me feel
Whole

Passion For Books

I hunger
For silence
I thirst
For knowledge
I've gained a
Passion for books
I wish I
Was in college
I dream to learn
All there is to know
Or at least
As much as my
Brain will let me
Hold in
I will not
Focus on the past
This is where
I'll begin

<u>The Name Of Pain</u>

She marked
Her body
Engraved in her skin
Is the name
Of pain
She has yet to
Entertain
That the name
Of this man
Will be the
Destruction
Of her heart
This man will
Rip her dream apart
Set fire to the
Passion in her
Heart
To leave her in
The hands of another
To piece back together

Answers To The Unanswered

Everything isn't
Written
Somethings elude
Even the human mind
Though in time
We will find
The answers to
The unanswered
There will always be
Life's little dampers
These small things
In our lives
That will put
A stamper
On our thoughts

Unforseen Illusions

My heart
My mind
Are caged
Trapped
In a place
Of unforeseen
Illusions
This intrusion
Has got me
Delusioned
About what my
Next move will be
I'll hold my
Ground and see
What circumstances
Bring to light
That which has
Eluded me

<u>Give Me</u>

Give me your pain
I will turn it into pleasure
Give me your sadness
I will turn it into happiness
Give me your weakness
I will turn it into strength
Give me your broken heart
I will cherish you forever

<u>Within Us</u>

Think of me
When the world
Tries to take your smile
Speak of me
Think of us
Because it's a must
That your beauty
Continues to shine
Speak of us
The life we will have
The hugs & the laughs
Our kids will bring us
From day to day
Dream of us
Because within us
There is love

<u>Lotus</u>

In the mud
I was birthed
In pain, in sickness
I arose strong
I blossomed, beautiful
The mud nurtured me
It nourished me
It was my salvation

No Beating

Constantly I look
Inside myself
Pain and anger
Still flows
Though no one knows
Of what my heart tows
I can no longer
Feel it beating
Can this be a greeting
That my end is near
I will no dwell
On this right here
I'll just play it
By ear
And continue to live
With no fear

From Father To Son

I just wanna build
My awareness
My own brand
Something great
For my young man
Give him something
He thought unseen
Something only visioned
Within his dreams
From father to son
This passion I have
To him i'll pass on
Anything is possible
Just to see the smile
On his face
To know he is happy
To feel his embrace

<u>Yours</u>

Your lips
So sweet
Your smile
Just glows
Your eyes
Glimmering jewels
Your skin
So silky
Your body
Dayumm sexy
Your look
As beautiful as
A queen gets

<u>Be Elusive</u>

How can I not
Focus on the future
My past was
So abusive
I've got to get away
Be so elusive
I didn't mean to
Be so intrusive
But I got to
Bust my way through
To get to a
Better future
Life has taken its toll
On this man
On this myth
I've been down
So many times
I no longer need a lift
Just a point
In the right direction
My pain is my protection
From any silly shit that came across
My path & try to infect it
I'm gonna keep going forward
Until my future is erected

She Brightened Everyday

How can I live
When the love
Of my life
Is gone
In the night
She brightened everyday
Now she will never
See the light
This here
Just can't be right
The tears flow
I'm gone
Out of sight

<u>Outro</u>

No matter what may get in your way or what obstacles you may have to face, just keep on flowing. Let no one tell you that you cannot do something or that your dreams are not possible. You can be anything you choose to be. Hard work pays off..